COLLEGE DROPOUT TO DIGITAL NOMAD

TOP 50 HACKS TO CREATING YOUR PASSIVE INCOME LAPTOP LIFESTYLE

ALEXIA KAZ

By reading this document, the reader agrees that under no circumstances is the author responsible for any losses, direct or indirect, which are incurred as a result of the use of the information contained within this document, including, but not limited to, — errors, omissions, or inaccuracies.

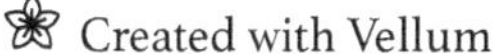 Created with Vellum

To my mom & aunt

My 2 superwomen

"Always follow your dreams and listen to your heart."

- Paulo Coelho

INTRODUCTION

Hey! By purchasing this book, you have made the first step of your passive income laptop lifestyle journey, so I want to say congratulations. You've done more than most have. The most significant hurdle in starting entrepreneurship is deciding to start. And, you started. You should be excited! I know I'm excited to be starting this journey with you.

A brief background about myself: I'm Alexia Kaz, and I've been an entrepreneur since the age of 7. I started selling my legos on eBay and haven't slowed down since. I've sold everything from phones, collectibles, clothing, jewelry, and video games; you name it. I've always had my hands in 20 different jars. I ran a reselling business while playing club soccer, basketball, flag football, and being a student. Soccer was a daily constant, so I continued to play and earned a Division I scholarship. That college experience was short-lived, however, as you can see from the title of this book!

After leaving school, with the tremendous encouragement of my mom, my world began to expand in ways I could have never imagined. I started my agency, traveled to 2 continents, met some fantastic people, tried new foods, experienced new cultures, and enjoyed experiences that weren't even on my mind's radar. I'm not saying this to brag whatsoever. I want to show you how expansive my world has become once I committed myself to the entrepreneurial journey. I've become a digital nomad!

When my world concentrated on one activity, it was very challenging to explore other avenues. However, after giving myself permission to trust my gut and leave what was no longer fulfilling me, I've had the freedom of a lifetime.

Why am I writing this? I know how much a college education is valued in North America. However, it isn't the only route. If you want to go to college and have that experience, then great! If you don't, then great! There are infinite ways to become successful, and you don't have to go along with the crowd. I gave up my scholarship, soccer, and college, which to many was ridiculous, but all that mattered was the belief I had and have in myself. I'm on a different path, and it's a beautiful one!

You can begin this journey at any age with any education. I'm a 21-year-old college dropout and am now the author of a book. I'd say that's a testament to everything I've been saying. The only obstacle was my mind preventing me from believing in that. The same goes for you. I'll say that again. The only obstacle is **your** mind stopping you from believing in that.

This isn't a book about doing one thing and getting rich overnight. I'm not in the business of scamming people, as I want to teach others the tools that have helped me open my mind and expand my world.

If you're skeptical, I get it. I was too. But why not permit yourself to try the hacks I share with you? You owe yourself that much!

So, all I ask from you when reading this book is that you keep an open mind. You bought a book from a college dropout, so keep that train going! You will see changes if you implement just a few hacks into your everyday life. Entrepreneurship is an investment in yourself.

We will review everything from self-care and mindset to reselling tricks that cost **$0,** hidden gems on the internet, and some incredible life-changing knowledge found in great books.

Okay, I'm ready to get started already, are you? Let's get into the Top 50 Hacks to Creating Your Passive Income Laptop Lifestyle!

1

MINDSET & SELF CARE ARE EVERYTHING

et's talk about self-care. Nothing can be accomplished without the power of maximizing your mind and self. This may be a book on passive income hacks, but we must check our minds, body, and self before anything can be accomplished. More people should take this seriously. How can you achieve great success without prioritizing your self-care? You can't. You can try, but an imbalance in the rest of your life would be present. Prioritize feeling good, and you will reap the benefits. Treat yourself like you would a best friend. I like to call it the best friend test. How would you take care of that best friend?

Hack #1 Exercise:

Millions talk about it, yet so few make this a priority. I'm not saying to run a marathon every month. Although you totally can. Walk 20 minutes daily, run 10 minutes, do some pushups, swim, or play basketball! There are infinite ways to boost your physical health. Try sticking to an exercise routine for a week. It doesn't matter how small and see how you feel after. This is the first step to creating a disciplined practice that will set the tone for the next steps of your entrepreneurial journey.

Hack #2 Meditation:

I know what you're thinking. I can't sit still for 10 minutes, let alone 5! I thought the same until I made it a precedent to try out meditation for a week. So I did just that, and yes, it was hard at first; thoughts would swarm my mind, but I stuck with it. It is now a part of my morning ritual. I can't go a day without it! I don't want to go a day without it. Meditation has such a misconception as "thinking about nothing for the whole meditation and being perfectly still and peaceful." Not true! Meditation is about letting those everyday thoughts surface and being okay with them being there. The more you practice this, the easier it will be to let them pass like clouds. You don't have to follow every thought that arises. Mediation is training that gives you the tools to calm your mind. Now tell me how that isn't related to business. Of course, it is!

Hack #3 Sleep & Make Your Bed:

I will keep this one short and sweet. Get a good amount of sleep. I will not bore you with statistics on why sleep is vital for your mind, body, and Soul because it just is. Everyone had a rough night's sleep and suffered the consequences the next day. So, prioritize your sleep because it matters. Also, make your bed. It is a simple 2-minute task that sets the tone for the day. Get a good amount of sleep and make your bed.

Hack #4 Hydration:

Growing up, adults always said, "make sure you hydrate!" Sometimes we did, sometimes we didn't. But they were right. Do you know how much water you drank today? Go fill up your water bottle and chug some water. I'm serious! Just like a lack of sleep, our bodies need water. So make sure you drink enough water every day, period.

Hack #5 Sobriety:

This might be a controversial hack to get behind, especially if you are a heavy drinker or smoker, but a genuine commitment to this hack will reap many benefits. Now that you have committed to implementing exercise, meditation, sleep, and hydration into your daily routine, imagine what being clear-minded about substances would do to your creativity. No more hangovers, distractions, or wishing you didn't say or do that one thing. I'm not saying don't have a drink ever again, but as I said at the beginning of this journey, try it and see the benefits that will come.

Hack #6 Journaling:

Have you ever journaled before? Not for school, work, or filling out a doctor's sheet. I'm not talking about those kinds of situations! But have you ever sat down and expressed your emotions on paper? I used to write occasionally, which was fine, but it wasn't until I committed to journaling every night before bed that I saw the impact. I slept much better because I got out all the thoughts circling my mind. With a clearer mind, I slept at ease and spearheaded my productivity the next day, the next day, and the next day.

Hack #7 Goal Setting:

Again, this might be commonly said to do, but do you do it? Do you write down everything you want to accomplish? These can be short-term or long-term goals, but the more specific you get, the better. There is a difference between a dream and a goal, and putting the actual energy of writing down what you want to accomplish differentiates the two. Everyone can have dreams, but admitting the goals you have for yourself by writing them down, and affirming them, has incredible rewards.

Hack #8 : Affirmations:

This hack is an excellent transition from #7! They are each other's glue. Along with putting the energy behind your goals, you must also put in the belief. I view belief as a mindset you can build, and affirmations are the key to that training. Affirmations work incredible wonders. I will get into this in the later chapters, but there is an excellent book with beautiful affirmations. Anyone can have a good idea, yet the belief system separates ideas from becoming successful businesses.

Hack #9: 5 AM Club

The title of this hack might scare some people. I know this concept scared me initially. Hearing all kinds of entrepreneurs preach, "waking up early" went in one ear and out the other until I did it. I committed to waking up early for a week, and wow, I accomplished a TON. I was up when many were still sleeping. That concept alone gave me energy. The early bird gets the worm! There are 24 hours a day; work with time instead of against it.

Hack #10: Cold Showers

Like Hack #9, I was very anti-cold showers for a while. I had heard about it but never implemented it. Now I crave the feeling of the cold running down my body. Like meditation, I took on this new training and now have another tool to calm my mind. How cool is that? Free training that anyone can do! Plus, it will save you some expensive hot water bills while you're at it.

Top 3 Hacks from Chapter 1

We discussed these first ten hacks, as they are the most important to creating your desired lifestyle. Nothing in your financial life can be in balance if your mindset and self-care are out of whack. Why do you think so many "successful" and so-called "made-it " employees drink and do drugs like crazy? There must be an imbalance in their self-care. You should do all of these hacks! But if you want to start small, which is okay too, these 3 are a must. I can't stress the importance of Hack #2, Meditation, Hack #8 Affirmations, and Hack #9, The 5 AM Club enough. Getting in alignment with your mind starts with being okay with your mind. Start meditation training, repeat affirmations daily, wake up before anyone else, and you will see how this new commitment spearheads your entrepreneurship journey. Now let's transition to making that money.

2

RESELLER IDEAS: SELL STUFF & MAKE MONEY NOW!

Reselling is best if you want to start making that first stream of passive income. The amount of items in your home, apartment, or storage you **barely** use is astronomical, and cash is waiting to be made. Let's jump right into things to see how we can get started!

The following four platforms have made me over $40,000 + in my lifetime, and I was just a seven-year-old kid when I started. I don't know what will happen if that doesn't grab your attention! When beginning to resell, eBay, Depop, Facebook Marketplace, and Craigslist are go-to's. This chapter will explore which platform to use for each item!

Hack #11: Clean Out Your Closet - Depop

This may seem like a no-brainer, yet how many clothes do you accumulate? Do you buy it and wear it once? I've been guilty of this many times until I discovered Depop! An app founded in the United Kingdom that sells to customers globally. I've sold anything from name brands to unbranded simple-looking shirts. The trick was marketing it correctly. The excuse "I don't have any nice clothes to sell" doesn't work with Depop. You can list almost any clothing on Depop, and it has the potential to sell. That is, with the right keywords. Finding the right keywords is simple! Download the app, create an account, and start looking at what other successful sellers are writing on their posts. Let's say you have a hoodie you want to sell, and it's unbranded. It doesn't even have a tag size. Well, guess what? That doesn't matter on Depop! Look up hoodies on Depop and note the description keywords that are attracting a ton of likes. From there, snap a few pics, insert the keywords that make this item attractive, weigh it on a scale (or make an educated guess), and through the very user-friendly app, you're listening will be up like that! The more items you list from your closet, the more mula you will be printing! Download Depop!

Hack #12: Collectible Coffee Mugs (Starbucks): eBay

I'll keep this one short and sweet because it's precisely what the title says. Believe it or not, some coffee mugs, specifically Starbucks Collector Series Mugs, are worth good money. When writing this, in May 2022, if I open the eBay app and look up the most expensive Starbucks mugs that recently sold, I see a Turks and Caicos 2017 Global Icon Collectors Series Mug that sold a few months ago for $541.00! For a mug! And I see countless others listed for higher. In other words, watch for Starbucks mugs if you want to make $500 + bucks on eBay.

Hack #13: Grow Plants to Resell

Many people enjoy getting their hands dirty, so why not make that profitable? The best part about this is that you don't need a huge garden or backyard to make it happen. It's crazy how little cost is required to start. Let's break this down. A pack of 15 plant seeds on amazon is under $10 bucks, soil on the lower end can cost anywhere from $4-$7, and a pack of 10 plant pots costs $13! So, all these can cost under $30 to create between 5-10 plants. Water them & watch them grow! There is a massive market for plant reselling. You can do this from the comfort of your driveway or on Facebook marketplace. Depending on the type of plant, they can go anywhere from $10-$30 each! Let's say you sell 7 out of the ten plants; that's $30 bucks pure profit. Can you imagine planting 100 plants? If you haven't noticed a theme in this book yet, I will say it loud and clear. If you commit to something long enough, you will see results.

Hack 14: Sell Coffee at the Park

It sounds exactly as the hack title says. Grab a large thermos, some black coffee, any coffee table in your home, small cheap dixie cups, and maybe some sugar, and there you go! You now have a small coffee stand in the park. This can work for cold or hot climates, as coffee or iced coffee is always a go-to. Charge a couple of bucks a cup, and the profits will add up quicker than you realize.

Hack 15: Sports Cards...

Sports fan or not, you or someone you know has some old sports cards from the past. It's worth that short text message to an old friend to find out. This is a quick hack, as it's pretty self-explanatory. Spend the 5 minutes seeing if you have any sports cards that may be worth money. You never know the value of something until you look it up!

Hack 16: Toner, Even Expired!

This is an incredible hack as many people throw away this cash cow, and I've seen them go on eBay anywhere from $40-$90, a single open box! Again, this is worth double-checking before you throw cash in the trash.

Hack 17: EMPTY Designer Boxes...Phones, Head-phones, Car Manuals!

It's crazy to resell an empty box for cash, but it works! Go in your closet, see what open shoe, bag, headphone, or apple boxes you may have, and hop on eBay to see what they are going for. Even if you don't have any empty boxes, offer to take them off your friend's hands for free! They will most likely be more than happy to give you what they think is trash, but you are becoming an entrepreneur, and you know better now!

Hack 18: Huge Book Stacks...

Many websites pay money to buy your old books. Of course, some books are worth more than others, and you won't be getting a ton of money individually, but it all adds up. Double check eBay as well because your book could go for more on ebay compared to what a wholesale book buyer offers. Do your research!

Hack 19: Go to Garage Sales & Flea Markets

Now that you have some re-selling hacks under your belt, it's time to be proactive and find some flips! Please give yourself a $50 limit; it could be less or more. I spent around $30 on clothes at a flea market, and I ended up netting about $500 in sales. You don't need to break the bank to do this! Go out and be determined to source some great hidden treasures.

Hack 20: Have a Garage Sale (Use Craigslist/Facebook Marketplace to Advertise)

You may have accumulated some extra stuff from your fun as a reseller. No worries! Hop on Craiglist & Facebook Marketplace, advertise your garage sale for free, wake up early the next day, lay out the stuff you want to sell, and make some cash in no time.

Top 3 Hacks from Chapter 2

That was a lot! We covered a ton of great places to start with your reselling journey. You can start with the least cost-demanding one and go from there. All reselling is fun, so it's hard to choose. However, if I had to narrow it down to 3, I would say **Hack #11: Clean Out Your Closet - Depop, Hack #16 Toner, Even Expired!,** and **Hack #17: EMPTY Designer Boxes...Phones, Headphones, Car Manuals!** All of these hacks are great options to start. You can walk over to your closet after this chapter and pick out at least five articles of clothing that you never wear. You may remember that you had that old iPhone box or some expired toner a neighbor was about to throw away. Just get started! I hope the juices are flowing in your brain with the excitement of reselling.

3

PASSIVE INCOME STREAMS THAT COST $0 DOWN

et's jump right into things. This chapter is all about ways to make money online that cost **$0 down.** You heard that right. Nada! Nothing! Zilch! No excuses but to put your head down and commit to at least one of these hacks.

HACK #21: Craigslist Free Section

We discussed Craigslist in the last chapter, but only for advertising your garage sale. There is more to discover! Craigslist has a free section on their platform where local people list items they are giving away. Sometimes you can find scores! Check the free Craiglist section every day for two weeks, and you might be amazed at what free items you can find for a flip.

Hack #22: Checkealos

A platform will pay you to test websites and leave feedback; this is a straightforward approach to making an extra $10-$30, depending on the length of the test. Take that 1 hour you would have spent watching Netflix and do two tests. That will pay for your lattes next week!

Hack #23: Etsy

Calling all creative people, this one's for you! Even if you don't view yourself as creative inherently, you picked up this book and want to learn more ways to enhance your life, so I respect your point, but I can't entirely agree with it. You are creative! Expanding your mindset IS creative, and Etsy is a great platform to do just that. You can sell anything from the art you love to create to fun cards, stickers, costume jewelry, or detailed notes!

Hack #24: Language Transcriber

This option is fantastic. However, you must check your state guidelines, as some don't allow this side hustle. But, if your state does, this is a great option to make some extra cash. Many websites will pay you to transcribe different languages, and you don't even need to speak that language with all the technology online to help you do so.

Hack #25: Paid Surveys

Countless websites will pay you to take a survey. As I've stated before, everything adds up, even in small increments. Paid surveys are simple and a great asset while waiting in line at your favorite grocery store.

Hack #26: Focus Groups

Like paid surveys, focus groups usually offer a higher paycheck to do! There are many options to do this in person and over Zoom nowadays, and it's a double whammy as you get paid and can potentially meet other interested digital nomads!

Hack #27: Teach English

VipKid is just one website that will pay you $14-$20 to teach English. Like being a transcriber, you don't need to speak other languages to do this, as VipKid fully immerses its students in English. Do your research to see which platform suits you best!

Hack #28: Dog Walker...

Many neighbors in your neighborhood probably don't have the time to walk their dogs. There's an opportunity here! Offer to do that for them! One client will turn into two, and the power of word of mouth will work from there.

Hack #29 Recruiter!

Some companies will pay job recruiters an insane amount of money to find a prospective job applicant! Many might think you need prolonged training to do this; however, at Ignite Recruit, that isn't the case! This is the Uber of Recruiting. As their CEO is a friend of mine, I know how incredible this opportunity is for anyone. You don't need to make it a full-time job, as many other recruiting companies require that. Check out Ignite and see the massive commission you could be making. All it takes is a committed mindset to stay consistent.

Hack #30: Be a Tour Guide for Your Neighborhood!

Have you grown up in one place and known it like the back of your hand? Or have you moved around and been privy to many places in the world? Go on TripAdvisor or Airbnb and create a listing as a tour guide. It's a fun and well-paying gig, and you could meet new potential business partners.

Top 3 Hacks from Chapter 3:

It's cool to think about how much opportunity there is, and it's just waiting for you to open your eyes. The top 3 hacks that are a must from this chapter are **Hack #21: Craigslist Free Section, Hack #25: Paid Surveys, and Hack #29: Recruiter!** The craigslist free section is a fun cash cow if you can commit to it. Paid surveys are easy and can be done at any point, waiting in line, at the airport, or waiting to pick up your kids. I think my favorite is Ignite Recruit. Just as Uber wasn't targeting taxi drivers to use their app, Ignite isn't targeting traditional recruiters! Anyone can do it and earn uncapped commission potential. Opportunity is everywhere! How fun is this!

4

HIDDEN GEMS TO SUPPORT THE LAPTOP LIFESTYLE

Do you want to up your passive income game? These options, from apps, to travel hacks, will continue to build your portfolio onward and upward. Let's dive right in.

Hack 31: Neighbor

The next generation of storage units brings you, Neighbor. This platform allows you to rent out space in your home, apartment, or backyard for a monthly charge. Do you think you don't have any extra room to rent? No worries! You could even make a little space in your closet and rent that out. This option is very user-friendly and worth running around your house to try and find some extra room to rent for fun!

· · ·

HACK 32: House Sitting

People will pay you to house-sit! How Passive does that sound? House sitting is unique because you usually won't be paid in cash but rather in amenities. So, bring your laptop and work on all the new passive income projects you've started since opening this book! And, you can stay in hundreds of different places, living rent FREE. This is the bread and butter of the laptop lifestyle.

HACK 33: Stash

Have you wanted to start investing in stocks but always thought it would cost too much? Stash is an investment app that can be broken down into fractional shares! Start with a $5 investment, and Stash will give you anywhere from $10 to $30 to invest in your portfolio! This is a great stepping stone to building your stock portfolio.

HACK 34: Inbox Dollar

If you already watch youtube videos or Netflix that take off hours of your day, you have to check out Inbox Dollar! Trade 30 minutes of that video binging and get paid to watch videos online instead.

Hack 35: Grabr

This app is just so neat! This app can be a massively helpful tool if you love to travel internationally or domestically. Many places have higher taxes in their country/state than yours so they may request an item cheaper in your location than theirs. After making the purchase, you will be reimbursed, plus your delivery fee, once you deliver it!

Hack 36: Indeed

Indeed is a beautiful platform to apply for online or in-person jobs. Hint: I will encourage online jobs, as you can work from anywhere! Now that you are developing your portfolio of money-making assets start searching the web of Indeed to see how you can make even more money!

Hack 37: My Points

As humans, everyone needs to buy groceries, soap, dishware, clothing, and other types of necessities. You can earn rewards while doing so! My Points is a phenomenal platform for earning points in multiple shopping genres.

Hack 38: Uber Eats & DoorDash

Having a car is such an asset these days. I can't even begin to unwrap all the ways you can make extra income with it. Uber Eats and DoorDash are great options as you are in charge of your schedule. Go on the app when you want to make extra money, and exit the app when you are done for the day!

Hack 39: Turo

Following the theme of using your car as an asset, Turo is another excellent avenue. Instead of using your car, you can rent it out to others! Let's say you are about to go on a week-long vacation and want to make some money while you're away. Start using Turo!

Hack 40: CashForDiabetics

This is a very market-targeted hack. However, I would like to include it not only because it brings awareness to diabetes but it can also help people who struggle with diabetes to make some extra cash! If you have leftover diabetic testing strips, this platform will pay you to send them your extras.

. . .

Top 3 Hacks from Chapter 4:

What a fun chapter! There are many creative ways to make extra cash, so I hope I'm not overwhelming you. Just one step at a time, or in better words, one hack at a time! My top 3 hacks from Chapter 4 are **Hack 31: Neighbor, Hack 35: Grabr, and Hack 37: My Points.** Find some extra space in your backyard or closet. If you are going to travel or do so for work, Grabr is a great way to make some extra income. And truthfully, we all need to feed and clean ourselves. My Points will give you additional benefits for your necessity shopping!

5

KNOWLEDGE IS POWER & THE BEST ASSET ONE CAN HAVE

I put this at the end of the book because of how crucial this chapter is. I wouldn't say I liked reading in school. The schooling system doesn't make it fun, and the books we read were not laptop lifestyle themed. It wasn't until I got recommended one book that set me on this knowledge-seeking path that changed my life. Books are the lowest-costing investment that has the highest ROI. I wholeheartedly believe that. It's an asset no one can ever take away from you. If you leverage books correctly, you will become a life-long learner regardless of college! Enough chit-chat already! Let's talk about books.

Hack 41: The Untethered Soul by Michael A. Singer

This book was recommended to me by an incredible friend, Ciara. I wanted tools to quiet my mind because, surprisingly enough, I hadn't ever been taught this in school. Singer lays out what it means not to get swept away whenever a thought arises. The voices in our minds are like noisy neighbors living rent-free! If you were walking on the street and someone was talking to themselves nonstop, how normal would that look in society? Our minds do that all the time! Singer gave me tools to work with my mind for the first time—a must-read.

Hack 42: Rich Dad Poor Dad by Robert Kiyosaki

This is a great intro book to financial education and having money work for you. I remember being unable to put this book down and feeling inspired to make passive income. Kawasaki also has a fun game called Cash Flow that teaches you how to escape the rat race 9-5!

Hack 43: The Power of Now by Eckhart Tolle

Similar theme to the Untethered Soul, this book you will want to read a couple of times. Each time I read this book, I gain new insights. My whole life, I've always wanted to "be present," but again did not have the tools to do so. To be present is a form of training, much like meditation. Through this book, you can add valuable knowledge to your mindset.

Hack 44: The 4 Agreements by Don Miguel Ruiz

This is a fantastic quick read on four moral agreements everyone should hold themselves to. Ruiz talks about the moral standard one should have when treating yourself and others. Self-care and care for others are mutually exclusive, and you have to take care of one to care for the other—a great book.

Hack 45: How to Win Friends and Influence People by Dale Carnegie

This book always turns people's heads by the title! It's a great addition to enhancing your people and leadership skills while bringing awareness to remembering people's names and letting others speak. Too many people cut others off mid-sentence, which is my pet peeve. This book is excellent training for that.

HACK 46: You Can Heal Your Life by Louise Hay

Louise Hay may be my favorite author. This extraordinary woman cured herself of cancer through the power of affirmations. Don't believe me? Okay! Read the book and see for yourself! I have seen many personal and professional improvements since implementing affirmations daily.

HACK 47: Ikigai The Japanese Secret to a Long and Happy Life by Hector García

Another quicker read, Ikigai, takes place in one of the world's blue zones! If you don't know what that is, blue zones are locations where the population statistically lives the longest. It's on my bucket list to hit all of them! In the blue zone of Okinawa, Japan, García mentions the Japanese word "Ikigai," which roughly translates to your "reason for being." Raising the question, what brings you joy in life? The book describes how many Japanese members of Okinawa still work until their hundreds because they love what they do. Ikigai is a feel-good piece of writing that encourages finding what you love and making it your job so it never feels like work.

· · ·

HACK 48: Untamed by Glennon Doyle

Untamed was one of the first books that showed me the true meaning of self-love and sexuality. Doyle touches on trusting oneself instead of living up to everyone else's standards. This a great book on female empowerment that men especially should read!

Hack 49: The Celestine Prophecy by James Redfield

I hadn't known what synchronicity meant until I read Celestine, and oh, how my whole world became so much more prominent after doing so. Redfield teaches us that coincidences don't exist and that the world is full of adventure if you allow it to be.

Hack 50: The Alchemist by Paulo Cohelo

I have read this book four times and counting. This was my first "book" love—an incredible story of a shepherd who sacrifices everything to fulfill his destiny. Paulo illustrates that each human has their own personal legend. We are on this earth to fulfill our destiny and life purpose. The Alchemist paints a beautiful story of tapping into our destiny!

. . .

Top 3 Hacks from Chapter 5:

Do you know when parents would refuse to pick their favorite child? I get it now because that is how I feel about this chapter! I love each of these books dearly. Seriously! I've had deep insights when reading these books that have shifted my mindset. You know I want you to read all 10, but if I had to choose three, they would be **Hack 41: The Untethered Soul by Michael A. Singer, Hack 46: You Can Heal Your Life by Louise Hay,** and **Hack 50: The Alchemist by Paulo Cohelo.** These three books are worth the small investment because the wonders you will experience after reading them will be infinite.

6

THE BONUS CHAPTER

30 HACKS PICKED UP IN 2022

I can't believe it's been almost a year since publishing College Dropout to Digital Nomad: Top 50 Hacks to Creating Your Passive Income Laptop Lifestyle. Wow, do I have some more hacks to throw your way! With almost 365 days worth of trial and tribulation, I did my absolute best to narrow it down to my top bonus 25 hacks to have in this chapter. I intentionally put each hack here, seeing them as golden nuggets that have helped me scale my agency and passive income laptop lifestyle to 6 figures by age 21. I don't have a college degree, and you don't need one, either. Are you ready for this? Let's dive in!

. . .

HACK 51: Chat GPT

Let's start this chapter off with a bang! If you have yet to live under a rock, you will have heard of Chat GPT by now. It falls between the lines of terrifying and brilliance with how much you can do. Think of anything you could do manually, but that has the potential to be done at 100x speed. I'm spitballing here, but if you want to start a business proofreading papers, have Chat GPT do it. If you are in college (not for long!) and hear your friends complain about a problem, find a way for Chat GPT to solve it. That's what entrepreneurship is all about. Finding a problem and then offering a solution! The end of your college road is coming, and people need a resume, but no one wants to make it themselves or know where to start. Boom. Here lies an opportunity. Offer them to make it yourself and have Chat GPT do it. Your friends will be so amazed at how fast you delivered this result that they will tell their friends, and then you can start charging people for this service. I took about 5 minutes to brainstorm those two examples. Imagine if you took 5 hours exploring all the ways you could make money with Chat GPT!

. . .

HACK 52: (SAAS) Software Flipping

I love this concept because you can get your ROI extremely fast. SAAS, also known as software as a service, is when you invest in software once and then leverage it repeatedly as your service. I'll give you an example. Canva. They are a great example. You invest in the platform at about **$12/month**, the price of 2 iced vanilla lattes in SoCal, and can create a beautiful itinerary for your neighbor's week vacay in the Bahamas. Charge them $50, and you will have made your money back for the month with just one sale and some profit. Now do that ten times, and you will have turned $12 into $500! This is one example of money, my friends.

HACK 53: Points Hacking

Have a credit card? Start booking business-class flights using your reward points. I booked a one-way business class ticket to Bali, Indonesia, in the heart of summer, using just points from my sign-up bonus. With taxes and fees, I ended up paying around $100; however, that would have easily been a $5,000 + ticket otherwise. With a credit card, you can maximize your rewards in countless ways. Julia Menez is my points coach and offers excellent free tools and courses. I highly recommend checking her out!

HACK 54: Bumble Biz

I am introducing a hidden gem out there regarding lead generation. Bumble is known for being a dating app; however, inside the app, there is a business section: Bumble Biz. AK Infinite has generated over **$40,000** using this platform. It works. We've tested multiple methods and have spent over 540 + days constructing our systems. If you want the step-by-step template we use for lead generation, don't hesitate to email me at lexi@akinfinite.com or set up a call with the team on the AK Infinite website!

HACK 55: Bali, Indonesia

Before going to Bali myself, I had heard nothing but great things. Everyone I spoke to mentioned the magic it held in the air. I need to check it out and see for myself! I showed you above how you could get there by paying less than **$150** for a ticket. However, you can make it happen, make it happen. Everyone should go to Bali at least once in their life. It had the same effect on me that everyone else spoke so highly of. The Balinese people, the kindness, the beauty, the water, the jungle, the animals, the ex-pats, the mopeds, the creativity, the excitement, and the list goes on and on. Go to Bali!

Updated Book Hacks

Hack 56: Expert Secrets by Russell Brunson

Russell is an expert marketer. His story is not only relatable to me, as he was a college athlete and expressed that he did not have time to dive deep into entrepreneurship. After reading Expert Secrets, there is no way you won't be filled with inspiration to take action. If you don't know how to market or what marketing is, read his book, and you can apply it to any business idea.

Hack 57: $100M Offers by Alex Hormozi

Okay, let me be upfront with you. If you don't know who Alex Hormozi is, please start now. He might be the most intelligent businessman alive. His companies do million-dollar weeks, if not more. I've read this book 2x and need to read it repeatedly. It's a playbook, and he has lost it all multiple times and rebuilt using these exact frameworks. What would you do with million-dollar weeks?

HACK 58: The 5 AM Club by Robin Sharma

I know the 5 AM Club hack appeared earlier in this book; however, I recommend reading Robin Sharma's engaging novel first. It follows a storyline of 2 individuals who aren't very keen at first to be waking up at the crack of dawn. I could relate heavily! It wasn't until I read this story that I understood the advantage waking up before the sun would give me.

HACK 59: Helping People Buy by Steve Lentini

Simply put, I was not too fond of sales. But as an entrepreneur, this was a skill I knew I needed to improve if I wanted to grow my business. I approached every sales call similarly, thinking, "how can I close this person?". No wonder I didn't enjoy sales; I was going through the motions! I didn't realize I wasn't listening in most conversations.

Instead, I was reading from a script. Steve's book completely reframed my mindset toward having conversations with people. How do you listen to your friends? How do you provide value in discussions? Regardless of whether you have a business yet, I believe everyone can advance their skillset of empathetic listening.

HACK 60: Playbook It!

Hack 60 is not a book to read, but how you can soak more value after finishing one! At the end of 2022, I will write down my notes and highlights from each chapter whenever I finish a book. Books are excellent investments in knowledge. However, if you don't apply what you learned from the book, then what is the point? I'm starting to see why we would write book reports in school once done reading! Please write down your takeaways, and watch how it sticks in your brain like a tattoo. On top of that, you can always go back to your notes and refresh your memory. It becomes your playbook.

BIZ STANDOUTS HACKS

. . .

HACK 61: Loom

Everyone is in each other's DMs these days. How can you stand out? Personalized Loom videos are the way. Loom is a platform that records your desktop screen while capturing your face in the corner. This tool alone has helped me close countless clients, as it showed the time I took to review their websites and provide some feedback. Again, how can you stand out when everyone is sending mass messages nowadays? Loom is the answer. On top of that, you get notified if the viewer has viewed your video. Whether you use this hack to impress your mom or a potential new client for your business, they both will stand out! If you want to see a real-world example of myself using Loom to sign a new client, contact me at lexi@akinfinite.com.

HACK 62: Hyperise

Piggybacking off of the "How can we stand out?" talk comes the platform Hyperise. Being a newer software, Hyperise is just scraping the scene as of February 2023. The number of conversations that have begun because I sent someone a Hyperise is astonishing. Essentially, you can create a photo or GIF one time using Hyperise, and then you can integrate it into your google chrome so it will personalize the name of the person you are messaging. Create once, scale indefinitely. Since using this, we believe our open rate increased by almost 10% - 15%! Metrics aside, sending someone a personalized GIF that you can repeatedly use at scale is another point of differentiation.

HACK 63: Notion

I'm a sucker for organizational tools! You could say the objective of Notion is similar to notes or google docs: to organize your busy life. However, with Notion, there are tons of integration to build schedules, and itineraries, color coordinate, ask AI questions, have dropdown/toggle menus, invite team members, and more. I use Notion for client roadmaps, trip itineraries, and weekly personal tasks; there are infinite ways to leverage this tool.

HACK 64: Lucidchart

If you are a visual learner, this is calling you! If you organize your mind, you organize your life, and business comes next. This platform lets you structure your workflows, thought processes, systems, and more into visuals. Robin Sharma speaks of this in his books and podcasts. One of his great tips is to "Blueprint" your weeks ahead. Take 1 hour or less on Sundays to map out on Lucidchart a blueprint of what you'd like to accomplish for the week. Start with a 30,000-foot view, then separate your work, personal, and spiritual, and from there, you can build out action steps for each category. Acting only as an example, feel free to do whatever is right for you! Lucidchart is free for the first three documents you make, and here's a hack within a hack; similar to google sheets, you can make another page within the document, so you don't need to pay for unlimited.

Hack 65: Lead Magnets

If you focus on providing value over everything else, then there's no way you won't be able to make money. People don't always buy because of the price but rather the value they believe they are getting. Let me illustrate an example for you. Let's say you love crystals. You've read multiple books and articles on crystals, listened to interviews and podcasts, and conversed with your friends on crystals. You feel pretty confident with your knowledge of crystals. Here's what I would do if I were you. Use the above hacks to build out a lead magnet to give away for free to pique interest and provide pure value. Create a Notion PDF that breaks down the top 10 crystals to buy for easing anxiety as a college student. From there, create a Loom video reviewing the PDF and send it to 10 friends, family, or people in your circle that you know like crystals. Or better yet, join 10 Facebook groups for crystal lovers. However, this will only work if you put great intention into your lead magnet. Don't just put some random 10 crystals. When you provide pure value first, people will start to think, "Well, if I got this for free, I can't image what I could get if I paid!"

MENTAL & Inner Health

HACK 66: The Medical Medium & Celery Juice

I got pretty sick in 2022. Multiple bacterial gut infections, countless antibiotics, lost weight, ended up in the hospital in another country, and the cycle repeated for a few months. I'm not saying this to complain, as I am okay, safe, and healthy now. However, this was an opportunity for me to learn about my health. I refused to take the 4th or 5th dose of antibiotics as it wasn't working. The Universe sent me my now-good friend Anthony one day while I was working at a coffee shop. He's helped me countless times, and I am beyond grateful for him. One of the best tools he gifted me was the Medical Medium. I learned about the powers of celery juice, cutting out eggs, the 3:6:9 liver rescue cleanse, and much more. Not only did I find an alternative way to heal my gut, I now have tools I can apply forever. If you can't tell by now, I love having tools, as I believe that is the best way to navigate life's journey! Even if you don't have bacterial infections, anyone can benefit from educating themselves on the powers of cleansing your gut. Do you feel fatigued sometimes? Crappy after eating specific foods? Trouble sleeping? Anxiety? Acne? Depression? Sadness? Please check out the Medical Medium.

. . .

HACK 67: Lemon Water

Quick segway from Hack 66 comes lemon water. From doing the 3:6:9 cleanse, which you don't have to jump to right away, I've built this into a habit of drinking lemon water first thing in the AM before eating anything and last thing before bed. The hydrating lemon water will cleanse your liver of the day's meals and consumption in your gut. Please do it for a week and let me know how you feel! Again, another tool to stay hydrated and fresh.

HACK 68: The Greatest Asset We Have

I don't remember where I picked up this beautiful quote, but it says, "Money replenishes, time doesn't."

PLEASE TAKE a second to think about the power of that. Whether you earn a paycheck, are on a scholarship, have passive income streams, or work a 9-5 job, this concept applies to everyone unless you've figured out how to add more time in a day! My point is this. Time is a finite asset we all have, so if you catch yourself making excuses of "I'll do it later" or "now is not the right time," I want to ask you, when will it ever be? Take action now. The hardest part is starting.

HACK 69: Money As An Energy Exchange

The title speaks for itself. Over this past year and 1/2 since leaving university, I've realized more than anything that the exchange of money is an exchange of energy. Many business owners I've spoken to might have good products or services. Still, I feel their success is directly correlated if they have a good attitude and relationship with money. If you see it as this ugly, greedy thing that never works out for you, it will see you like that too. Or, if you see building wealth as a privilege and responsibility that you get to do while helping people and providing value, then that will be reciprocated within your work. As my mom says, everything is an inside job. Every morning, I say, "Wealth and Abundance come to me effortlessly." I'm constantly building my relationship muscle with money as I believe it's a live entity. Does having a negative relationship feel good? Why not try another way?

. . .

HACK 70: Extreme Ownership & Devicelessness Hour

I'm unsure if I made up a word with "devicelessness" right there, but let's run with it! *Mi mejor amigo* Atilio recommended this incredible book to me. Two navy seals break down what it's like to be a leader who takes extreme ownership of everything they do. Whether you are a soccer coach, teacher, student, business owner, janitor, pizza maker, or mother, this applies to you. Do you feel frustrated with the way things are sometimes? Your team isn't performing how you'd like them to; your kids keep fighting; you are overwhelmed with your workload. Well, it starts with you. I can relate if you said yes to any of the above questions. A little bit ago, I was frustrated with the results of my team as I felt I gave them all the tools, SOP, and documents they needed to be successful, as it worked for me. Once stumbling on "Extreme Ownership," I quickly realized there was so much more I could be doing. If I was frustrated with the results, what could I do better to make the training more cohesive? How could I spend more time communicating with my team, reviewing SOPs, and improving the systems? Even though the tools I initially gave them worked for me, one size does not fit all. Ever since practicing extreme ownership, I've set aside 1 hour (non-negotiable, no one can get in touch with me) every day when my phone is turned off, and I either journal, reflect, or read about how I can take extreme ownership.

HIGH TICKET GAME Changers

HACK 71: Maria Wendt

Maria has extremely affordable courses you can get instant access to. She gives you tips, tricks, and systems for generating leads from Instagram, building a Facebook Group, growing an email list, launching a $10K campaign, and more. She's a great introduction to the Universe of online courses. You can find some of Maria's courses at www. mariawendt.com

HACK 72: AIA

Shoutout to the Mickelson twins, who have taught me so much about building a publishing empire! Their course has taught me how to self-publish the book you have in your hands and create a cash flow machine of a passive income! They will teach you how to find an undersaturated keyword on the Amazon kindle bookstore and create an outline for a ghostwriter to write your 30,000-word book. I published my first 30,000-word book in November of 2022, and at the time of writing, this brings in about $1,500 in pure royalties. That's just from one book. Wait till I publish 10! Check out their course at www.publishing.com

HACK 73: Modern SDR

Not only does my great friend Kekoa run this program, but I've firsthand worked with him on staffing SDRs, so I can vouch for what he's built. Modern SDR is an excellent avenue if you don't necessarily want to start running your own business immediately but learn from other business owners who will put you into their ecosystem right away. Modern SDR illustrates being a digital nomad, as you can do this from anywhere with a laptop or cell phone and a wifi connection. Checkout Kekoa's program at www.themodernsdr.com

· · ·

HACK 74: Click Funnels

From the author of Expert Secrets comes the CEO of Click Funnels, Russell Brunson. He gives this example in the book, so I will do my best to summarize it here. Have you ever been to a drive-through, and after you order your hamburger, they ask you if you'd like fries and a coke to go with it for a special bundle discount? Even though you never mentioned the fries and coke in your original order, they offered it to you after you ordered. Essentially, this is a funnel. An upsell. Companies do this all the time! I bet you will start to see this everywhere now that I've pointed it out. It's genius marketing, especially if you put a one-time discount deal with those fries and coke. The person ordering will feel like they are getting their money at a discount if they agree to add the fries and coke to the order because it's cheaper than buying separately. Marketing at its finest, as the drive-through, factored into their profit margins by adding this type of bundle discount. The world of Funnels is vast, so don't worry if you feel over-whelmed. I was when I first dove in. I'd start by watching some YouTube videos on "What is Click Funnels" to see if they pique your interest!

. . .

HACK 75: Business Ownership Accelerator

There are over 4,000 + unique and different franchises across the United States. It's not just the mainstream Mcdonald's and Chic-fil-A that exist. One of my clients and friends, Keith Liscio, offers a Business Ownership Accelerator where he analyzes if owning a franchise makes the most sense for you. I've not seen anyone else position their services as Keith does. He doesn't charge anything up front; instead, he provides value on what he believes could benefit his client's the most. His offer encapsulates everything I discussed above by delivering value, and the rest will follow. You can check out his company at www.excelsiorfranchisecenter.com

CONCLUSION

I am so proud of you for completing this book! Every hack means something special to me, and I hope you feel the time and intention behind each one. Anyone can do this, but your belief in the process separates you. Yes, it can be challenging, and there are unknowns, but all you have to do is start! Pick a hack from every chapter and COMMIT to it. You will see changes with commitment, belief, and consistency.

Don't ever give up on your passive income laptop lifestyle because it won't give up on you. Everywhere you turn in entrepreneurship, you will see opportunity. I'll keep this short and sweet as you have some work now! I am so excited to see where life takes you along this journey.

Please keep in touch, and if you found this book helpful, please leave a favorable review on Amazon! And remember one thing: Money don't sleep. Only you do.

xx

- lexi

BIBLIOGRAPHY

A. (2023a, January 13). *Home - The Modern SDR*. The Modern SDR. https://www.themodernsdr.com/

AK8. (n.d.). https://www.akinfinite.com/

Brunson, R. (2017). *Expert Secrets: The Underground Playbook for Creating a Mass Movement of People Who Will Pay for Your Advice.* Morgan James Publishing.

Bumble | Date, Chat, Meet New People & Network Better. (n.d.). Bumble. https://bumble.com/

ClickFunnels<sup>TM - Marketing Funnels Made Easy. (n.d.). <span>https://www.clickfunnels.com/

Geobreeze. (2023, January 29). *About Me - Geobreeze.* https://geobreezetravel.com/about-me/

Hay, L. (2017). *You Can Heal Your Life 30th Anniversary Edition.*

Home | Publishing.com. (n.d.). https://www.publishing.com/

Home - Excelsior Franchise Center. (2021, December 9). Excelsior Franchise Center. https://www.excelsiorfranchisecenter.com/

Hormozi, A. (2021). *"00M Offers: How To Make Offers So Good People Feel Stupid Saying No.* Acquisition.com.

https://www.canva.com/. (n.d.). Canva. https://www.canva.com/

Hyperise: Grow conversions with personalization of your images, videos and website content. (n.d.). https://www.hyperise.com/

Lentini, S. (2021). *Helping People Buy: If You Hate the Word "Sales", You will love this book!*

Loom: Async Video Messaging for Work. (n.d.). Loom. https://www.loom.com/

Lucid. (n.d.). *Intelligent Diagramming | Lucidchart.* Lucidchart. https://www.lucidchart.com/

Make Money & Get Clients Quickly with Maria Wendt. (2001,

September 2). Make Money & Get Clients Quickly With Maria Wendt. https://www.mariawendt.com/

O. (2023b, February 2). *ChatGPT: Optimizing Language Models for Dialogue.* OpenAI. https://openai.com/blog/chatgpt/

Sharma, R. (2018). *The 5 AM Club: Own Your Morning. Elevate Your Life.* HarperCollins.

William, A. (2020). *Medical Medium Cleanse to Heal: Healing Plans for Sufferers of Anxiety, Depression, Acne, Eczema, Lyme, Gut Problems, Brain Fog, Weight Issues, Migraines, Bloating, Vertigo, Psoriasis, Cys.* Hay House, Inc.

Willink, J., & Babin, L. (2017). *Extreme Ownership: How U.S. Navy SEALs Lead and Win.* St. Martin's Press.

Your wiki, docs & projects. Together. (n.d.). Notion. https://www.notion.com/

Ebay: Starbucks Collector Series Mugs. (2022). eBay. Retrieved May 14, 2022, from https://www.ebay.com/sch/i.html?_from=R40&_nkw=starbucks+collector+series+mugs&_sacat=0&_sop=16&LH_Auction=1&rt=nc&LH_Sold=1&LH_Complete=1

My Points: Shop. (2022). My Points. Retrieved May 16, 2022, from https://www.mypoints.com/shop-featured

User Experience Testing Platform - Checkealos. (2022). User Experience Testing Platform - Checkealos. Retrieved May 16, 2022, from https://www.checkealos.com/get-paid-for-your-feedback/

Ferguson, E. (2022, January 14). *24 Best Side Hustle Ideas to Make an Extra $1000+ a Month in 2022.* Shopify. Retrieved May 16, 2022, from

https://www.shopify.com/blog/side-hustle#25

Hanna, H. R. (2022, March 24). *21 Sites That Will Pay You to Test Out Websites.* The

Work at Home Woman | Legit Work From Home Jobs. https://www.theworkathomewoman.com/test-websites/

We Buy Diabetic Test Strips for Cash. (2022). Cash For Diabetics. Retrieved May 16, 2022, from https://cashfordiabetics.com/?

alid=miol2reymirre4&utm_source=LP&utm_campaign=side-hustle&click_id=102453f08894cb76d890a319b4d9db&utm_medi um=&utm_term=GoogleAdWords&utm_content=%2Fways-to-make-extra-money&lpx=v1

Neighbor. (2022). *Neighbor | The Cheaper, Closer & Safer Storage Marketplace.* Retrieved May 16, 2022, from https://www.neigh bor.com/search?can_store_vehicle=false&length=10&max_ size=300&search=Santa%20Monica%2C%20CA%2C%20USA& width=10

InboxDollars® - the free online rewards club that pays cash. (2022). InboxDollars. Retrieved May 16, 2022, from https://www.inbox dollars.com/?cmp=2124&cxid=0-%2Fways-to-make-extra-money&aff_sid=1025fbc7aef7963d5662992bd78635

Frankel, L. (2021, December 10). *How to Make $100 a Day - 17 Simple, Legit Ideas.* FinanceBuzz. Retrieved May 16, 2022, from

https://financebuzz.com/how-to-make-100-dollars-a-day?utm_ source=financebuzz-extra&utm_medium=email-es& utm_term=oim-sh&utm_campaign=7760&clickid= 147c15d3e0f677f1e4c3dc4792a6e7fa&utm_content=9539&affid= 2&email_segment_id=&aff_unique3=10416

Amazon.com: Set of 15 Black Duck Brand Heirloom Flower Seeds 15 Different Varieties Non-GMO - (Variety Deluxe Flower Garden) : Patio, Lawn & Garden. (2022). Amazon. Retrieved May 16, 2022, from

My Book

I made over $1500 in 4 hours selling plants from my home driveway!! Here's how I did it. (2021, April 10). YouTube. Retrieved May 16, 2022, from https://www.youtube.com/watch?v=_HxZdCvDAcY

Amazon.com: Miracle-Gro Potting Mix 16 qt : Everything Else. (2022). Amazon. Retrieved May 16, 2022, from My Book

Amazon.com: 10 Pack Mini Terracotta Pots with Drainage Holes for Plants, Succulent, Cactus (1.5 in) : Patio, Lawn & Garden. (2022). Amazon. Retrieved May 16, 2022, from My Book

Earn $14-22/hr teaching English online. (2022). VipKid. Retrieved May 16, 2022, from https://www.vipkid.com/teach

Razinski, S. (2022, April 4). *Paid House Sitting Jobs: 12 Sites That Pay You to Stay Home.* Ivetriedthat. Retrieved May 16, 2022, from https://ivetriedthat.com/paid-house-sitting-jobs/

Indeed Job Search. (2022). Indeed. Retrieved May 16, 2022, from https://search.indeed.jobs/main/jobs?keywords=&location= united%20states

Ignite Recruitment | United States. (2022). Ignite Recruitment. Retrieved May 16, 2022, from https://www.igniterec.com/

THE 10 BEST Los Angeles Food Delivery & Takeout - Order Online from THE BEST Restaurants Near You | Uber Eats. (2022). Uber Eats. Retrieved May 16, 2022, from https://www.ubereats.com/ city/los-angeles-ca

DoorDash Food Delivery & Takeout - From Restaurants Near You. (2022). Door Dash. Retrieved May 16, 2022, from https://www. doordash.com/

Turo Car Sharing Marketplace. (2022). TURO. Retrieved May 16, 2022

Sell Your Books and Sell Back Textbooks At sellbackyourBook.com. (2022). Sell Your Book Back. Retrieved May 16, 2022, from https://www.sellbackyourbook.com/?gclid= CjwKCAjw7IeUBhBbEiwADhiEMXgfNVKs9RFQY7ZgnC_m LvKpAbPPuVDoMqyem4GoMuFKiFiPfsddiBoC64QQAv D_BwE

Singer, M. A. (2012). The Untethered Soul: The Journey beyond Yourself

Kiyosaki, R. T. (1997). Rich Dad Poor Dad: 20th Anniversary Edition: What the Rich Teach Their Kids About Money That the Poor and Middle Class Do No. Brilliance Audio.

Eckhart, T. (2022). *The Power of Now.* Hodder & Stoughton.

Ruiz, D. M. (2003). *Wisdom from the Four Agreements (Mini Book) (Book and Access ed.).* Peter Pauper Press.

Carnegie, D. (2022). *How to win Friends & Influence People* (100th Printing ed.). SIMON & SCHUSTER.

Hay, L. (2017). *YOU CAN HEAL YOUR LIFE / TRADE.* Hay House Inc.

García, H., Miralles, F., Avila, O. L., & Audible Studios. (2019). *Ikigai: Los secretos de Japón para una vida larga y feliz.* Audible Studios.

Doyle, G., & Melton, G. D. (2020). *Untamed* (Later Printing ed.). The Dial Press.

Redfield, J. (2018). *The Celestine Prophecy* (Reissue ed.). Grand Central Publishing.

Coelho, P. (2014). *The Alchemist: 25th Anniversary Edition* (Anniversary ed.). HarperOne.

Craigslist. (2022). Craigslist. Retrieved May 16, 2022, from https://losangeles.craigslist.org/

Depop. (2022). Depop. Retrieved May 16, 2022, from https://www.depop.com

Facebook Marketplace. (2022). Facebook Marketplace. Retrieved May 16, 2022, from https://www.facebook.com

Stash. (2022). *Stash | Investing for Beginners.* Retrieved May 16, 2022, from https://www.stash.com/

Shop Overseas Products with International P2P Delivery. (2022). Grabr. Retrieved May 16, 2022, from https://grabr.io/en/